Henry's Just a Chuckle

excerpted from

By Henry W. Haverstock

We Need To Laugh More so we don't surrender to the harsh realities seen in a dynamically changing world. The strain of daily living in the 1990s needs to be met with a Positive Attitude and an ability to laugh at life's absurd moments. In fact, laughter promotes good health and builds emotional bridges. Like music, laughter is a Universal Language. *continued on page 64*

Henry's Just a Chuckle
by Henry W. Haverstock

Copyright © 1992 Henry W. Haverstock

All rights reserved. No part of this book may be reproduced in whole or in part, without written permission from the publisher, except a reviewer who may quote brief passages in a review showing the logo of the cover on any page showing the quoted oneliners; nor may any part of this book be reproduced, stored in a retrieval system, or transmitted in any form or by any means electronic, mechanical, photocopying, recording, or other, without specific written permission from the publisher.

Many jokes excerpted from *Henry's Hilarious Oneliners* © 1990 by Henry W. Haverstock. Additional new jokes © herein.

Cover Art and Illustrations by Barry Lawrence
© 1991 Henry W. Haverstock
Text Design & Book Development by
Robert Parker & Associates
and Laser Set of Minnetonka

HENRY'S HILARIOUS ONELINERS is a trademark of Henry's Publishing Company Inc.

First Printing, May, 1992
ISBN 1-879916-09-6
Library of Congress Catalog Card Number 91-90330

Ladies and Gentlemen,
Children of All Ages...

Welcome to fun and humor by my close friend and associate, and namesake, Henry my man.

As The One and Only LAUGHING MOUSE, I, Henry of Hopkins, seek nothing more than for you to be joyful and happy. And from time to time when you find it in your heart to leave a little cheese around, I would be most appreciative.

The material contained in this book has been collected over many years from a variety of sources, often passed on to me by my associates, to be used in my various talks before clubs and business dinners. Many of the original authors are unknown, and some one-liners have been attributed to more than one author. Therefore, it is truly impossible to list each source. I would like for this to be an acknowledgment of appreciation to the authors for the thoughts, if not the words, of witticism contained herein.   *Henry W. Haverstock*

Dedication

To All Those People Who Love To Laugh

Introduction

Laughter is good for the spirit. Laughter promotes good health. The late Norman Cousins, in his book *Anatomy of an Illness,* showed how laughter in his own life helped him survive a near-fatal disability and extended his life for many years.

Increasingly, laughter is recognized as an essential element to a balanced life. In recognition of this, a new TV channel was recently set up for cable TV, devoted exclusively to funny, laugh-producing programming.

For many years—and without any particular system about it—I have enjoyed collecting what I considered funny one-liners. Some time ago, I decided to bring these random bits and pieces together. At the same time, I have been testing these one-liners before various groups in which I am active, including Rotary, Exchange Clubs, and the Y's Men's clubs.

I am happy to report that they usually bring a good laugh, though sometimes only a good natured groan—or, on rare occasion, hisses or boos.

Very little of my humor is original but much of it has undergone re-wording. This is due in large part to my inability to write as fast as the stories are told oratorically. With the printed word, this has not, of course, presented the same problem.

In any case, it will be for you, the reader, to determine whether my choice of one-liners produces for you, health-giving laughter. Since one-liners are short and generally easy to remember, I hope that you can use some of them to add interest and sparkle to all of your own social encounters.

Have fun.

Henry W. Haverstock
Minneapolis
March, 1992

1

Newspaper retraction: "Last week we noted that Mr. Jones was a defective in the police force. This was a typographic error. Mr. Jones is really a detective in the police farce."

2

They've developed a new insecticide that doesn't actually kill flies but makes them so sexy that you can swat them two at a time.

3

A dentist had a patient whose breath was so bad that he had to work on his teeth through his ear.

4

A wife told her husband that the car had water in the battery. The husband asked: "Where is the car?" She replied innocently: "It's in the swimming pool."

5

They have a telephone dial system for atheists. You dial a number and no one answers.

6

A Minister was conducting the funeral of a Deacon. In his eulogy, he pointed to the corpse and declared that the soul had left. "What you see here is just the shell; the nut has departed."

7

A Norwegian ice factory was forced to close when they lost the recipe.

8

Asked the young woman: "Do you think thirty years is too great a difference in age between a man and a woman when he's the President of a bank?"

9

A lawyer stayed up all night trying to break a widow's Will.

10

It was so windy the other day that a chicken laid the same egg four times.

11

He's as careful as a nudist climbing over a barbed wire fence.

12

The ten best years of a woman's life are between 28 and 30.

13

Lawyer to Judge: "Judge, my client stole the ring in a moment of weakness."
Judge: "I suppose if he had had a moment of strength, he would have stolen the safe."

14

The Norwegian government has been having trouble with its space program. Their astronaut keeps falling off the kite.

15

Mrs. Upton's dog has been run over. She will be heart broken. Don't tell her abruptly. "No, I'll begin by saying it's her husband."

16

"I hate my mother-in-law," said one cannibal to another at dinner. Responded the other: "Then, just eat your vegetables."

17

Recently, we heard of an Iraqi bookkeeper who absconded with the accounts payable.

18

A nurse was asked why she had a rectal thermometer behind her ear. "My goodness," she exclaimed, "now I remember where I put my ball point pen."

19

A doctor ordered a patient to have not more than one drink a day. The patient reported that he was following orders and was up to March 5, 1995. (This was March, 1989.)

20

He has such a big mouth that he can eat a banana sideways.

21

Sign on Chinese laundry: "We don't tear your clothes with clumsy machinery. We do it carefully by hand."

22

The average man's idea of a good sermon is one that goes over his head and hits one of his neighbors.

23

A man was so far down on his luck that he didn't dare scratch matches on the bottom of his shoes because it tore his socks.

24

A cannibal mother and her child saw an airplane fly over. Child to mother: "What's that?" Mother: "It's something like a lobster; you only eat what's inside."

25

Victor Borge: "I know only two pieces. One is 'Clair de Lune' and the other one isn't."

26

Message on fortune cookie: "Ignore previous cookie."

27

Marriage is the only war where you sleep with the enemy.

28

Ad in a New York paper: "Piano moving; expert handling. Careful moving a must with us. Also, kindling wood for sale."

29

A fireworks factory in South Dakota blew up with such an explosion that the city is now located in North Dakota.

30

Sign on car: Sex Appeal—Give Generously

31

A guide explained that the huge rock formations were piled up there by the glaciers. A curious old lady: "But where are the glaciers now?" Guide: "They've gone back to get more rocks."

32

Barber, to customer: "Haven't I shaved you before?" Customer: "No, I got that scar in the war."

33

Sign on back of truck in New York: "Help keep New York clean; dump your garbage in New Jersey."

34

The circus manager refused to let the human cannon ball quit, asking: "Where can I find another man of your calibre?"

35

The miracle drugs are marvelous. Now, a doctor can keep a patient alive until he pays his bill.

36

Two English ladies are talking at tea. First lady: "Breeding is everything, isn't it?" Other lady: "No, but it's lots of fun."

37

Any time a person feels lonely and neglected, he should think of Whistler's father.

38

It takes at least 48 rabbits to make a sealskin coat.

39

"I have 4 aces." "You win; I only have 3 aces."

40

You are getting old when you get winded playing checkers or you sink your teeth into a steak and they stay there.

41

An Indian girl married a Jewish boy. To please their unhappy parents, they name their first child WHITEFISH.

42

Ziggy, getting some pills from his psychiatrist: "And if these pills make you feel too euphoric, tune in the news."

43

A black man tried unsuccessfully a number of times to join a Southern Baptist church. The minister asked him why he quit trying. The black man said that he talked it over with God, and God said not to feel bad, that he himself had been trying to get in for 30 years.

44

Once, I threw myself on the mercy of the Court, and missed.

45

A leading actor in a play was surprised when the telephone on stage rang at the wrong time. Nonplussed, he picked up the receiver, turned to his co-star and said: "It's for you."

46

A Minneapolis business man, in seeking to make peace between Minneapolis and St. Paul proposed that the names be combined to Minnehaha: Minne for Minneapolis and haha for St. Paul.

47

In the Winfield, Kansas, *Courier:* "As an encore, Mrs. Brown played the old favorite: 'Carry Me Back to Old Virginity.'"

48

He sold me group insurance, but the whole group has to get sick before you collect.

49

Man, to girlfriend: "Those lovely soft hands," he whispered, "that hair, and those beautiful eyes—where did you get those beautiful eyes?" "They came with the head," the girl replied.

50

A man told his wife he wasn't drinking any more. He added *sotto voce* that he wasn't drinking any less either.

51

Two men discussing their new boss: "You can't help liking the guy; if you don't, he fires you."

52

My wife had an accident at the bank recently. She got in the wrong line and made a deposit.

53

Did the mudpack help your wife's appearance? It did for several days but then it fell off.

54

George Burns, to Playboy advisory staff: "I'd read your magazine more often, but my glasses keep steaming over."

55

A man was saying grace in a low voice. Somebody at the table said: "I can't hear you." The man replied: "I wasn't talking to you."

56

Sign in apartment building: "No baby carriages or foreign cars allowed in the lobby."

57

Driver, nearing Chicago, saw a sign which read: "Chicago Left"; so he turned around and went back home.

58

The Director of the Old Log Theater, on his newest highly successful play "Run for your Wife" said that "if you don't enjoy this play, we want you to come to the box office afterwards and we'll try to figure out what's wrong with you."

59

A Midwestern man referred to his New York mother-in-law as the wicked witch of the East.

60

Sign: "Save water, bathe with a friend."

61

A man, trying to lose weight, took up horseback riding. In the first week, the horse lost ten pounds.

62

Billy Martin was the only man in the world who could hear someone giving him the finger.

63

Jerry Reed song title: "She Got the Gold Mine; I Got the Shaft."

64

"Never accept a drink from a urologist."
                    Erma Bombeck's father.

65

Bowlegged cowboy, after completing Army physical: "Well, Doc, how do I stand?" Doc: "That's what I want to know."

66

Grand Forks, North Dakota, is not the end of the earth; but you can see it from there.

67

Groucho Marx: "Either this man is dead or my watch has stopped."

68

Professor: "This examination will be conducted on the honor system. Please take seats three seats apart and in alternate rows."

69

A rooster crows early because he probably figures he can't get in a word edgewise after the hens get up.

70

"How is your wife's driving?" Husband: "Last week she took a turn for the worse."

71

Lady in presence of her small son to waitress: "May I have a bag to take leftovers to my dog?" Son: "Oh, mother, are we going to get a dog?"

72

I take my children everywhere but they always find their way back home.
Robert Orbin.

73

Lady on witness stand, to cross-examining attorney in a bastardy proceeding: "What do you think I am?" The Attorney: "We've already established that. Now we're trying to determine the degree."

74

Maternity is a matter of fact; paternity is always a matter of opinion. J.C. Ridpath.

75

A psychiatrist had his office decorated with new furniture made of overwrought iron.

76

Woody Allen: "My wife was very immature. I'd be in the bathroom taking a bath and she'd walk right in and sink my boats."

77

Henny Youngman: "Some people ask the secret of our long marriage. We take time to go to a restaurant two times a week—a little candle light, dinner, soft music and dancing. She goes Tuesdays and I go Fridays."

Henry W. Haverstock, author of the most humorous and successful HENRY'S HILARIOUS ONELINERS, the first of a series of Henry's fun books. PHOTO CREDIT: ILGA CIMBULIS

Meet Henry's Namesake

Henry W. Haverstock has been a practicing attorney and real estate investor for over forty-five years. As a teenager he contracted polio, which led to paralysis and many years of recovery. He was the first regular patient in the United States of Sister Kenny, the renowned Australian nurse. He was able to learn to walk with crutches, and has kept a keen sense of humor that he has used continually.

Haverstock graduated from the University of Minnesota in 1945, and received a law degree from the University of Southern California. He helped create a radio show, "You and the Law," which he emceed; and he is a life member of Courage Center, Golden Valley, Minnesota.

He lives in a Minneapolis suburb with his wife Shirley, and presents one-liners to Rotary, Kiwanis, YMCA, Exchange, Optimist, and Lions Clubs. He inspires everyone with direct talk and laughter. Many of the letters he regularly writes to editors of American newspapers have been published and are the basis for a future book.

78

The difference between the Polish Mafia and the Italian Mafia is that the Italian Mafia makes you an offer you can't refuse and the Polish Mafia makes you an offer you can understand.

79

Johnny Carson: "Nancy Reagan fell down and broke her hair."

80

He was picked to be an astronaut because he had such a great sense of direction.

81

Secretary to boss: "I've got good news and bad news." Boss: "Give me the good news first." Secretary: "You're not sterile."

82

During the New Hampshire primaries, a baby had been kissed by so many candidates that she developed chapped cheeks.

83

A traveler returning to the United States from abroad was challenged by a customs agent as to whether he had any pornographic material. He replied: "I don't even have a pornograph."

84

Politician: "I sleep like a baby. I go to sleep for an hour, then wake up crying."

85

A teacher instructed the parent to get an encyclopedia for his son. The parent responded: "Nothing doing. He can walk to school like I did."

86

A young man who was engaged to four girls at the same time explained that Cupid must have shot him with a machine gun.

87

Boston Globe: "The font so generously given by Mrs. Smith will be set in position in the East end of the church. Now, babies may be baptized at both ends."

88

Mountain View (Calif.) *Pictorial News:* "Men's Activity Night starts March 25 in the girls' gym."

89

Waiter: "How was the soup?" "To tell you the truth, I'm really sorry I stirred it."

90

In Iowa, they have three grades of gas: regular, premium and whole wheat.

91

One Senator: "Senator James is his own worst enemy." The other Senator: "Not while I'm alive."

92

A man convicted of killing his third wife was asked why he cracked her skull. He explained that his first two wives died of eating poisoned mushrooms but his third wife refused them.

93

Student: "Why does the whistle blow for a fire?" His friend: "It doesn't blow for the fire, it blows for the water. They've already got the fire."

94

Henny Youngman: "If I'm not in bed by 11 p.m., I go home."

95

Calvin Coolidge: "When more and more people are thrown out of work, unemployment results."

96

Psychiatrist: "I wouldn't worry about your son making mud pies. It's quite normal." Mother: "I don't think so and neither does his wife."

97

A man's pajamas were so worn that when he sat down with a dime in the pocket, he could tell whether it was heads or tails.

98

A lady was endeavoring to cash a check at a bank. The cashier asked her if she had anything by which she could be identified. She replied: "I think so, yes; I have a wart on the back of my neck."

99

A man in northern Minnesota by the name of Charlie shot a loon and ate it for dinner. The local game warden, a friend, heard about this and went to him saying, "Charlie, you should know better than to shoot our state bird. It's illegal, and I'm going to have to fine you." After the warden fined Charlie $100, he said, "Say, Charlie, just out of curiosity, what does a loon taste like?" Charlie replied: "It wasn't too bad, kind of a cross between a bald eagle and a trumpeter swan."

100

A certain boxer, being terribly beaten and mauled, in going to his corner after a round, said his opponent never laid a glove on him. The trainer replied: "Well, you better keep an eye on the referee then, because somebody is beating the hell out of you."

101

A veterinarian and a taxidermist are considering merging their practices so that, either way, you get your pet back.

102

Exasperated man to his computer: "Do you understand the meaning of the word sledgehammer?"

103

A man caught a fish that was so big that the picture of it alone weighed 12 pounds.

104

Sportscaster after seeing a baseball player fall twice in the first inning: "He washed his legs today and can't do a thing with them."

105

A man wanted to get a skunk out from under his house so he put some lutefisk there. The skunk left, but the problem then became how to get the Norwegian out from under it.

106

Muhammed Ali: "My toughest fight was with my first wife."

107

For people who like peace and quiet, they've developed a phoneless cord.

108

Burns: "If I have a problem, I don't take it to bed with me. I tell her to go home."

109

Woody Allen was in a plane that was crashing. He said that a whole life flashed before him, but it was the wrong life.

110

Thomas Edison told of the Boston man who was waiting for a total eclipse of the sun so that he could send a telegram at the special night rates.

111

Olaf Johnson wears dark glasses around the house, explaining that it bothers him to see his wife work so hard.

112

In applying for a job where it asked the woman her age, one woman put down: "Nuclear."

113

An old maid spent 3 days at the airport getting frisked. What was so surprising was that she didn't even have a ticket.

114

A golfer got caught in a hurricane and made a hole in none

115

He carries pictures of his children and a sound track of his wife.

116

A minister left his church because of illness. His congregation got sick of him.

117

Said to a small person: "Good things come in small packages." Small person's rejoinder: "So does poison."

118

A familiar saying in the French Foreign Legion: "When in doubt, gallop."

119

A man has invented a sprinkling can without any holes in the spout for people who have artificial flowers.

120

Member of hunting party to guide: "I thought you said you were the best guide in Vermont." Guide: "I did, but I think we're in Canada."

121

Would you like your mother-in-law embalmed? Cremated? Buried? "That'll be fine."

122

A prostate operation is now called a low botomy.

123

A boy told his father that he was kept in after school because he did not know where the Azores were. Father: "Well, in the future, just remember where you put things."

124

Sheriff: "Did you catch the auto thief?" Deputy: "He was a lucky bird; we had chased him only about a mile when our 500 miles was up and we had to stop and change the oil."

125

Drunk to bar tender: "Hey, gimme a horse's neck." Second drunk: "I'll have a horse's tail; there's no sense killing two horses."

126

"And there, son, you have the story of your dad during the Vietnam War." "Yes, Dad, but why did they need all the other soldiers?"

127

Personally, I felt a lot more secure in 1933 when all I had to fear was fear itself.

128

Dean Martin is considering filling his swimming pool with martinis. He claims that that will make it impossible to drown since the deeper you sink, the higher you'll get.

129

Patient to psychiatrist: "I feel schizophrenic." Doctor: "That makes four of us."

130

A man comes to a psychiatrist with a cabbage hanging from one ear, a string of carrots around his neck and a bracelet of olives, and says: "I came to see you about my brother."

131

A doctor treated a man for varicose veins for six weeks, then discovered that the patient's fountain pen leaked.

132

Perfect timing: being able to turn off the hot and cold shower faucets at the same time.

My Favorite *Chuckles* Checklist

1 ☐	23 ☐	45 ☐	67 ☐	89 ☐	111 ☐
2 ☐	24 ☐	46 ☐	68 ☐	90 ☐	112 ☐
3 ☐	25 ☐	47 ☐	69 ☐	91 ☐	113 ☐
4 ☐	26 ☐	48 ☐	70 ☐	92 ☐	114 ☐
5 ☐	27 ☐	49 ☐	71 ☐	93 ☐	115 ☐
6 ☐	28 ☐	50 ☐	72 ☐	94 ☐	116 ☐
7 ☐	29 ☐	51 ☐	73 ☐	95 ☐	117 ☐
8 ☐	30 ☐	52 ☐	74 ☐	96 ☐	118 ☐
9 ☐	31 ☐	53 ☐	75 ☐	97 ☐	119 ☐
10 ☐	32 ☐	54 ☐	76 ☐	98 ☐	120 ☐
11 ☐	33 ☐	55 ☐	77 ☐	99 ☐	121 ☐
12 ☐	34 ☐	56 ☐	78 ☐	100 ☐	122 ☐
13 ☐	35 ☐	57 ☐	79 ☐	101 ☐	123 ☐
14 ☐	36 ☐	58 ☐	80 ☐	102 ☐	124 ☐
15 ☐	37 ☐	59 ☐	81 ☐	103 ☐	125 ☐
16 ☐	38 ☐	60 ☐	82 ☐	104 ☐	126 ☐
17 ☐	39 ☐	61 ☐	83 ☐	105 ☐	127 ☐
18 ☐	40 ☐	62 ☐	84 ☐	106 ☐	128 ☐
19 ☐	41 ☐	63 ☐	85 ☐	107 ☐	129 ☐
20 ☐	42 ☐	64 ☐	86 ☐	108 ☐	130 ☐
21 ☐	43 ☐	65 ☐	87 ☐	109 ☐	131 ☐
22 ☐	44 ☐	66 ☐	88 ☐	110 ☐	132 ☐

See pp. 54–59 for ideas on collecting your own jokes.

Clips, Cartoons, and Quips

The art of the joke as an important part of social interaction has slowly disappeared. Jokes are used mostly for entertainment on radio, television, and in professional publications; and often these are contrived and usually not as funny as those spontaneous situations and spoofs we do to each other in fun. Probably the decline in personal letter writing replaced by telephone talking is why jokes and one-liners are not recorded as often in written form, and people seem to be just more serious in their daily activities. Below I have listed the dictionary meanings for those parts of jokes and one-liners that can be developed from everyday experiences.

CLIPSHEETS (CLIPS) – *Sheets of newspaper stories, articles, and jokes to be saved. Usually placed on only one side of the paper.* Clip and save!

CARTOON(S) – *A drawing caricaturing some action or subject. A sequence of drawings relating to a comic incident or a story, often called a comic strip.* The best known of printed joke forms today, but usually produced professionally rather than by individuals for friends. At one time, many letters had one or more cartoons drawn in the margins by pen and colored inks.

QUIP(S) – *A clever or witty remark, usually sarcastic.* A quipster is the person who quips against others using verbal remarks.

CHUCKLING – *Softly laughing to oneself; Being amused.*

BELLY LAUGH – *A loud hearty laugh usually in an informal situation, but not always; and not required to have fun.*

ONE-LINER – *A brief, witty, or humorous remark, often written on more than one line, but spoken as if just in one continous form.*

HENRY'S ONELINERS – © copyrighted one-liners and jokes used in *Henry's Hilarious Oneliners* book and *Henry's Hilarious Postcards, Henry's Just a Laugh, Henry's Just a Chuckle, Henry's Just a Witticism.*

You Can Tell Your Own One-Liners

When you focus attention on the daily world around you at home, office, and even in shopping centers and at school, you can often see humorous situations and hear funny one-liners from the actual conversations. The problem is trying to remember them even when you repeat them several times to friends and family.

The answer is to write the words down carefully so you can actually repeat them months later. One-liners seem to change as you tell them to others: a word here, a phrase there, and you have a different statement...sometimes no longer funny. Try to keep the situation first seen and heard described simply in the words written. Jokes and humor often happen spontaneously. Don't trust yourself to remember without recording the words.

Use the space on the next page of this mini-book to start your collection. Better yet, look for *Henry's Hilarious Oneliners* in your bookstore. It has over 800 jokes plus pages that serve as your own personal humor scrapbook.

My Own One-Liners

You Might Become Published!

One-liners and humorous short tales that can make people laugh and be happy in this difficult and stress-filled world are heard locally in towns and cities everywhere, but often the best one-liners soon are lost to the rest of the world. You can help change that and get credit, too, for original one-liners.

Henry's Publishing Company is interested in exposing more people, especially office workers and business people, to the joys of a little chuckle or a hearty laugh to offset the serious side of daily business.

Send your ORIGINAL one-liners and jokes, heard or experienced by you, your family and friends to us at the address below, typed or printed very clearly. If we think it is funny, too, we will consider including it in a future one-liner book crediting your name, city, and state. No One-liners Will Be Returned and They Become The Property of Henry's Publishing Company, Inc. to be used solely at its discretion. Include your full name, address, and age (Those eighteen or younger, please ask one of your parents to sign a copy of the statement below).

Please, do not use one-liners from newspapers, magazines, or other printed matter. Those one-liners heard on radio or television originally should list the show, date, station, and people identified and involved. Do not send any one-liners or jokes heard on humor shows or specials.

Include this statement, signed and dated:

"I hereby give permission for my enclosed original one-liner and/or joke to be used by Henry's Publishing Company, Minneapolis, MN 55343, in any form, and release all rights to said company without payment."

_____

Your signature and date here.

Mail To: New One-liners
           Henry's Publishing Company, Inc.
           Post Office Box 5175
           Minneapolis, MN 55343

If we include your one-liner, we will try to credit each author with a listing. No Guarantee, but wouldn't it be fun to be published in a book?!?

LAW OFFICES OF
HENRY W. HAVERSTOCK

September 5, 1991

Hon. George Bush, President
United States of America
White House
Washington, D.C.

Dear President Bush:

    With so many grim events in the news on a daily basis, I submit that there is a need for a National LAUGHTER WEEK.

    Such a week might furnish a respite during which we could each take stock, and return to a more rational perspective—one which is slanted toward all the good in the world.

    Laughter is good for people. It enables us to build a more proportioned view of our lives, and that of our fellow man. Laughter, like music, is a universal language. Laughter, appropriately used, builds bridges between people. Laughter promotes health; it stimulates the health—inducing endorphins. Laughter enriches every relationship: business, social, political, recreations. More laughter might also mean less crime.

To get things going, I am enclosing a complementary copy of my new book, HENRY'S HILARIOUS ONELINERS. When you have stopped laughing at these one-liner jokes (One of your own appearing at entry 792), I am sure you will see the wisdom in allowing the whole nation—and maybe the whole world—in on the importance of laughter.

I suggest the week following the April 15 income tax deadline as an appropriate one to set aside for a whole week of tension-easing laughter, while we move back into life's everyday preoccupations.

Respectfully—and hilariously—yours,

Henry W. Haverstock

Henry W. Haverstock

If you've enjoyed this sampling of Henry's collection of personal and borrowed humor, you'll really like his original book of over 800 one-liners, *Henry's Hilarious Oneliners,* printed in soft cover and hard cover editions for your permanent library. And if you'd like to give someone special a mini-book version of Henry's whimsical assortment of comedy, there are currently three titles available: *Henry's Just a Witticism, Henry's Just a Chuckle,* and *Henry's Just a Laugh.* Tuck these mini-books into your pocket, purse or briefcase for a handy reference the next time you need a little punch for your conversation, speech or meeting. Ask for them at your local bookstore.

Henry's Publishing Company, Inc.
Post Office Box 5175
Minneapolis, Minnesota 55343

A Robert Parker & Associates Book

continued from page 1

Henry's Just a Chuckle gives you a laugh book, like a favorite list of songs and notes, to cheer and jeer, relaxing yourself, family, friends, and business associates—enabling everyone to get a better perspective on life.

The Quality of Life can be greatly enhanced by the use of jokes and one-liners, fun to most everyone present at a gathering of two or more, and bringing a chuckle or laugh to the individual reader. Often we forget the punch lines of jokes we have heard, or wish we had a way to make a friend laugh.

Henry's Just a Chuckle offers more than 100 jokes gathered over many years by Henry W. Haverstock. This book also describes methods of gathering your own one-liners and provides space to record new jokes you have collected. You will also enjoy other books in the series: *Henry's Just a Laugh* and *Henry's Just a Witticism*.